T0198983

EMPLOYEES ARE
FLOWERS

TESSA VINCENT

AuthorHouse™ UK
1663 Liberty Drive
Bloomington, IN 47403 USA
www.authorhouse.co.uk
UK TFN: 0800 0148641 (Toll Free inside the UK)
UK Local: 02036 956322 (+44 20 3695 6322 from outside the UK)

Because of the dynamic nature of the Internet, any web addresses or links contained in this book may have changed since publication and may no longer be valid. The views expressed in this work are solely those of the author and do not necessarily reflect the views of the publisher, and the publisher hereby disclaims any responsibility for them.

Any people depicted in stock imagery provided by Getty Images are models, and such images are being used for illustrative purposes only. Certain stock imagery © Getty Images.

This book is printed on acid-free paper.

ISBN: 978-1-6655-8812-6 (sc)
ISBN: 978-1-6655-8813-3 (e)

Print information available on the last page.

Published by AuthorHouse 05/06/2021

authorHOUSE®

EMPLOYEES
ARE
FLOWERS

About the Book

As basic as it sounds, one of the keys to business success is to nurture your employees. Does it happen always or even most of the time? No. This pocket guide will help you re-evaluate your working practices to incorporate humanity into your workforce and the benefits it can bring. Tessa Vincent has used the analogy of a flower to illustrate the concepts of her experience and theory. After all, we reap what we sow…

Contents

Introduction

I've asked myself why I need to create an analogy for human behaviours in the workplace. I feel that employers can tend to their gardens better than their staff because that is what's on show. So I have chosen to compare the management of employees to gardening. If you can grow a beautiful flower, then you can grow the best successful talent. We are not all born with humanitarian instincts, and so this book is designed to teach employers how to believe in the value of human life in the workplace environment. My theory is that making the employee happier—I mean, who really wants to hold the bad-guy card anyway?—leads to business success because of increased employee productivity. It really is a win-win!

This short but sweet book is designed to be a quick self-help guide for employers who are struggling with such issues as the inability to retain staff, low employee productivity, poor staff morale, and high absenteeism. For many employers, the starting point is that the employee is at fault, but this book will question the behaviours of the employer, the structure of the business, and how even slight changes in attitude and workplace practices in the way employees are treated can have profound effects. Happy staff equals productivity—in turn increasing profit.

My husband calls me "Mr Benn". For those of you who did not grow up in the UK in the 1980s, Mr Benn is a television character that had a different career every episode. Very much akin to the butcher, the baker, and the candlestick maker, I have been a qualified hairdresser, adult general nurse, and lawyer. I commenced my law degree in 2011 and have now settled in my position as a solicitor for the local government, but I have extensive experience working in a diverse range of industries.

I started part-time jobs around schoolwork at the age of 14, and since then I've held positions as a restaurant supervisor, barmaid, factory worker, retail assistant, and childminder, to name a few. I reached management level as a nurse specialising in fertility—oh, and now I can add author to the list.

My ethos is "if in doubt, throw it out"—which translates to, if you are not happy in your job and there is no prospect of improvement, then move on. Life is too short. In many instances, what I did not enjoy wasn't the work but the treatment of management towards me and other members of the team.

Commonly we see drained individuals, miserable and anxious even at the prospect of entering their workplace, who don't really grasp that life is for living and somehow lose the ability and zest to change their life. This book is meant as a wake-up call for employers through a take-no-nonsense approach for employees.

I am very attuned to the workplace environment from working in both skilled and non-skilled roles and professions. On every rung of the hierarchical ladder, I have witnessed the very best and the very worst of what a good employer should be. My unique insight of diversity in this field and the appalling human experiences I have witnessed others subjected to, have prompted me to write this book.

To conceal the identity of any unpleasant perpetrators I've encountered throughout more than 31 years of employment, I won't offer direct examples of unfavourable treatment towards me or others. Instead, the book will be very generic, and I will portray my experiences in a broader sense. Nonetheless, I will provide examples of excellent bosses I have encountered over the years and how their ethos has caused the workplace environment to blossom.

I've become a confident speaker over time—yet another hat I wear—and am available to hire for employment-related conferences or motivational speeches, sharing face-to-face what I have learnt from my experiences, in an effort to improve methods in managing and supporting staff—thus creating a happier workforce and a more profitable business.

Chapter 1

Foundations

I am not sure why some employers just cannot grasp the simple concept that what you put in you get out. It's like planting the seed. I have a feeling that managers—though not all—have overinflated egos, a sense of hierarchical power, and a tendency to take all the credit for the work of others. Often they have no management experience and have been promoted into this role because of their experience or skill in their chosen profession, which does not by default make you a good manager. Yes, by all means, managers need to have an in-depth grasp of the business product, but even more so a manager must be a people person. They should be natural around people and enjoy human interaction as someone who can communicate well and be culturally diverse. Ideally, the trait of altruism in a manager benefits staff well-being.

Some employers haven't liked me in the past; I tell it as it is and don't tolerate nonsense. Irrespective of our position, we are all equals in this world and deserve to be treated that way. We are also all cogs in the business machine, so even if your salary is lower than that of other members of the team or you have fewer qualifications, your role is still vital in the functioning of the workplace.

I have witnessed so many employers dictating to their staff, treating them poorly, not giving them adequate breaks, expecting them to work late but not be paid, and basically treating them as if they are worthless, to be honest. It is only human instinct as an employee to think, *Well, stuff this.* The life gets drained out of these employees, and as a result their motivation diminishes, they lose respect for their employer, their absent rate increases, and at some point, if they are wise enough, they will contemplate their life and leave.

Let's say, however, we look at the elements of planting a seed and what we need to achieve in order for a flourishing flower to grow. We prepare the soil, we plant the seed at the right depth, and we provide water, sunlight, and love. The results are clear.

How can we nurture our employees the way we want our flowers to grow?

First, the basics. In order for employees to work effectively, they need the right training, support, and tools. If they have just commenced employment, they must be trained correctly, even if you are at your busiest season. You must be patient; we all take things in within different time frames.

Second, get to know your employee. You don't have to be best friends with your employee—and in actual fact, it doesn't make good business sense to be. But you need to have a genuine interest in their health and well-being. Know your employees' children's names. Have a conversation with them that isn't work-related and show interest. It is cold and blatantly rude to know nothing about an employee's life; don't treat them like a number. Put yourself in their shoes and be empathetic to their needs. It's the right thing to do, but what's most important is that you actually care.

Third, find out what they need to grow, just as you would for the seed. Have regular meetings with each of your staff to ensure they all feel supported. Listen to their concerns and act on them. Listening without acting is fruitless. Ask if they are happy in their role, what they enjoy the most, and what you can do to make their working life better.

Don't be overly strict. Unless health and safety rules dictate otherwise, let them have their mobile phone on their desk. If they have to rush out because their child is sick, support them and don't make them make up the time. We are all human, and for a work-life balance we need to keep stress to a minimum in this hectic world. Trust me—employees treated fairly will repay you with integrity and loyalty.

Chapter 2

Love

Is it really that hard to show a bit of love and be genuine? Apparently so. If you don't have the requisites to be kind and compassionate, then I am sorry, but you should not be in charge of human beings. Human beings, like the seed, need love to grow. We are not robots and can't flourish in a world of neglect and mistreatment.

Don't make insinuating comments, don't gossip behind your staff's back, and don't push your staff to the breaking point. Think of a dishcloth: to rinse out the excess water, we twist it tightly until no further drops appear. Don't do this to your employees; be respectful and reasonable with workload capacities. Just remember it is not their company. Should you as the employer wish to work until the crack of dawn, then that's your choice, but don't expect or for that matter allow your employees to follow suit. The days of slavery are long gone, and so do not encourage this kind of behaviour.

Chapter 3

Open

We are all intuitive. It's not rocket science to realise when managers are talking behind your back. It creates a very cloak-and-dagger environment and a bitchy setting. We are not handmaids working at Gilead from *The Handmaid's Tale*! Gossiping and back-stabbing creates a toxic, traitorous, soulless environment. The hierarchical divide is enough to make the strongest of employees crumble. In the employee role in these environments, you really need to leave your personality at the door, get into your robot control suit, and suffer. At times over the years, I have found myself purchasing wine on the way home from work just to soften the blow from the painfully exhausting day—something I wouldn't ordinarily do. Allowing businesses to be driven by power junkies equates to unhappiness and poor staff morale that would bring a tear to a glass eye. I'm aware of colleagues who have seen their doctor for depression as a direct result of the way they have been treated at work.

If you do have a genuine issue—and I emphasise the word "genuine"—with your employee, then discuss it openly, honestly, and empathetically with them. Don't gossip behind their back with your peers. Have team meetings to discuss matters that have come to your attention in a productive and sensitive manner to find a sensible resolution. Don't think you are better than your employees just because you are in a higher position. Who gives you the right to belittle other people?

Many employers have the attitude that working for their company, in any industry, is the prime prize, but I am sorry to put it so frankly: if you want your employees to work their butts off to fill your pockets, it is a two-way transaction.

Coming from a health-care nursing background, I know the importance of work-life balance—fresh air, exercise, diet, downtime or family time—and the importance of this balance in maintaining our brain functionality and mental health.

We can see from OCED Better Life Index that a person's job can be the top denominator that controls their quality of life. Especially if we work full-time, we spend an incredible amount of time at work. If we get the right balance, we can be more productive and create better results, in turn increasing financial growth by working fewer hours when our brains and bodies are better cared for.

Sweden, for example, rates well; it is common for companies to offer flexible working, and on average only 1 per cent of Swedes work more than fifty hours per week. These incentives are used as leverage to entice the most talented, and I would wholeheartedly agree that these are contributors, my main theory being that the denominator of being human and kind-hearted is an equation for success. You attract the best employees, and they don't want to leave! It's only logical.

Working fifteen-hour days, but being obese, grabbing junk food at the desk, and not having any exercise or time with your family can only lead to family issues such as divorce, health problems, and a drained brain with production inabilities. Plus, we really don't want to lie on our deathbed with the realisation we put our job before our family.

We are all human, and some days we are just not going to be as productive as others. That needs to be accepted.

Where would *you* rather work?

Chapter 4

Workplace Practices

We have all experienced that feeling of utter dread when the alarm clock goes off on a Monday morning and it's time to face the reality of another week in a job that makes you feel anxious as soon as you reach the door.

You don't know if your boss is going to be smiling or tutting at their watch when you arrive at precisely 9:02 a.m. I have often said I would rather have a boss who is consistently horrible than a boss who is Mother Teresa one minute and Cruella de Vil the next.

Set a benchmark and stick to it. Be consistent. Of course, through management experience, a manager's skill is going to diversify, but at least decide on a model which creates a happy, stable, positive environment enabling the talents of staff to flourish without fear.

It is important and financially advantageous to put happiness and staff well-being into your business model. The worst thing you can do as an employer is to create an environment of backstabbing, unease, and fear.

Although in the business hierarchy managers are higher up the ladder than their staff, the biggest flaw they can have is to perceive themselves as superior on a personal level.

Overinflated ego is one of the ugliest character traits in the workplace—or in society in general, really. Their balloons must be swiftly burst by a very sharp pin, or this ego will end up being the company's demise.

Investing in your staff emotionally and through career development will ensure they feel like valued members of the team. Bitter, unfounded criticism does nothing for one's self-esteem. A business should promote positivism and mental well-being, and this in turn will boost staff morale.

Chapter 5

Equality and Ego

I have been very fortunate not to have witnessed or been subjected to any kind of discrimination on grounds such as race, religion, or pregnancy. Fortunately, under the Equality Act 2010, there are nine protected characteristics in Britain intended to prevent you from being treated unfairly on these grounds, including also disability and gender reassignment—which is not to say discrimination is not still a huge issue in our society and all over the world.

Everyone—blue, orange, or green; poor or rich; at the highest or lowest position—should be treated with the same dignity and respect. We are all born into this world the same way, and we will all die and leave the world in the same way. If there is one thing that I detest in life, it's snobbery.

Interestingly, in my experience bosses with overinflated egos are linked to a lack of productivity. I would like to take credit for discovering this dynamic, but shockingly, after typing "egos inhibit productivity" into Google there were about 5,100,000 results in less than half a second. Wow!

I can only work in an environment where I can be myself. I have my own mind and can't be controlled. Of course I exercise this independence under the remit of my role, but I've had trouble in the past when bosses have tried to mould me into something I'm not.

Those in senior hierarchical power positions may dictate in an old-fashioned, Edwardian head-teacher style. The workplace may be akin to prison life, where staff are treated like a number and not a human-being. The employee is spoken to in a blood-curdling and gut-wrenching tone. They are made to feel worthless, and the toxicity that radiates from the overinflated ego or superiority complex is almost unbearable in the atmosphere. It's like the employer treating their staff like glass robots then hurling bricks at them until they shatter into tiny pieces.

It would be interesting to analyse the statistics of the onset of mental health issues directly attributed to verbal abuse and pressure at the hands of one's employer.

So why do overinflated egos inhibit productivity? For the same reason that I can't work in an environment where I feel controlled. If we are controlled, we cannot let the flower blossom. We stop the sunshine and rain that grows the seed. If we are controlled, we can't express our ideas, and we are frightened to engage because we know we will be offended or belittled.

Components of success are being open-minded, curious, inventive, and innovative. If your boss wants to look the smartest and have the best ideas, they are going to stagnate the company by dismissing and inhibiting the ideas and views of others.

Those with a superiority complex do not praise others because they want all the praise and attention for themselves. When we learn to accept ourselves with our faults and abandon the need of approval from others, the world opens and shines so much brighter. We need to be receptive to the ideas of others and welcome positive change. I cringe every time I hear "but this is the way it has always been done."

Chapter 6

Reality

I don't live with my head in the clouds (if only!) and think that life is a bed of roses. I am aware being a manager is not easy and not all employees are good seeds capable of growing into beautiful flowers if nurtured in the right way.

We have all experienced that one employee who just wants to stir up trouble and causes all sorts of unnecessary grief. I do believe nonetheless that everyone deserves the opportunities to succeed. I believe that every seed needs to be given the same care, love, and attention, and there is no room for favourites in the workplace.

We have to be realists, though, and recognise when our seeds are just not growing the way we hoped. Just as the toxic manager destroys the crop, so does the toxic employee. You do not need a weed trying to twist around and destroy your beautiful roses. The weed will dig deep into the soil and corrupt your garden. The weed has to be removed, and the gardeners out there know that some weeds can be really stubborn. Their roots seem to dig deeper than one could ever have expected, and they cause all sorts of damage to the flowers around them. It is the task of managers to man up to these toxic employees, who we all know can be intimidating and even intimidate the managers. Legal procedure needs to be followed to dismiss them through the correct channels.

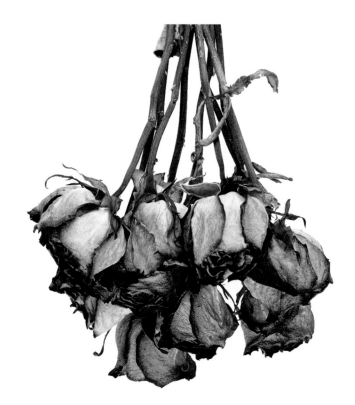

I have seen managers scared of other managers, and managers scared of staff members. This is no use. We can't have managers who are wimpy daisies. A manager who tolerates the unruly behaviour of another manager or a staff member, scared to rock the apple cart, is allowing the weeds to spread and maybe even fertilising them.

Have a measurement tool for productivity. In my opinion, time is not a good measure of output. I have seen employees work long hours to gain brownie points but really achieve very little. They are drained, grab unhealthy snacks, don't look after their health, and just want to look good with their lights still on in the office at all hours. I have seen other employees work their contracted hours, undertake regular exercise, eat healthy, and produce far better results than the former.

As I have a nursing health background, I do not agree with working all hours of the day and night, which leads to a work-life imbalance. I like to perform my work to a good standard, but the only way I can achieve this is if I care for myself physically and mentally. I need time to spend with my children and get fresh air and make healthy choices. I can't possibly do this if I must work until 1 a.m. Realising this as a manager is crucial. If your staff burn out, your flowers are going to die in the heat. Set realistic work goals and expectations for your staff. Don't overload them. If they end up off work with stress and fatigue, or encounter emotional worries as their spouse and children never see them, then as well as losing a valuable member of the team, your business is ultimately going to suffer.

Chapter 7

See

One of the keys to success is homing in on the unique skills of each individual. We all have strengths and weaknesses, and we are all so different. Why not measure the key strengths of your employees and channel these skills to meet your business needs? *See* the qualities, uniqueness, and strengths in your staff and utilise these to benefit your business and their professional development.

When I was nursing, there was a care assistant who had a passionate interest in wound care, which was more the role of the qualified nurse. But our manager recognised the carer's capabilities. The carer was trained up and because of her unique interest quickly became the go-to person for advice on wound care. She diligently researched wound care because she was grateful for the opportunity and responsibility the manager had placed on her. It was statistically recognised in the care home that the wound healing rate had risen since this carer had been appointed that role. A lot of other managers would have said no, feeling unprepared to train this girl because she was not a qualified nurse.

That manager was diverse and seized an opportunity to reap enormous benefits, both economically (wound care products are expensive) and in terms of the well-being of the patients (such as less pain and more mobility).

Some people are clearly better at communicating than others. Promote these people to positions that involve dealing with clients or the public.

I find this works best when Employees are interested in a specific dynamic of their role. See your employees for who they really are, what are their likes and dislikes. Don't mould them into what you want them to be; mould them into the best version of what they want to be. You can't change a blue flower to a pink flower. You need to let the flower grow to be the very best version it can be, and you can do this only by supporting it, nurturing and loving it, and letting it flourish at its own pace.

Conclusion

We are all human, and we are all, both employers and employees alike, going to have good and bad days. That is part of life.

We also of course are going to bond better with some people than with others. But I think we need to be realistic about the fact that none of us are or ever will be perfect, and accepting that makes life so much easier.

We will all make mistakes, but we need to be more considerate, compassionate, and loving to one another. Pointing the finger or being mean does not benefit any business environment. You need to look for solutions, not problems, and work as a team, embracing one another's qualities.

Printed in the United States
by Baker & Taylor Publisher Services